Ring of Fire

Ring of Fire

A TRIBUTE TO JOHNNY CASH

BRIAN MANSFIELD

Photographs by LES LEVERETT

RUTLEDGE HILL PRESS®

Nashville, Tennessee

A DIVISION OF THOMAS NELSON, INC.
www.ThomasNelson.com

For Zach,
who considered Johnny Cash his hero,

and for Annalise,
who shared a few hours on this earth with a great man

Copyright © 2003 by Rutledge Hill Press.

Published by Rutledge Hill Press, a Division of Thomas Nelson, Inc.,
P.O. Box 141000, Nashville, Tennessee 37214.

Photos on pages 67 and 79 by Libby Leverett-Crew. All other photos by Les Leverett.

Book design by Gore Studio, Inc. | www.GoreStudio.com

Library of Congress Cataloging-in-Publication Data is available.
Mansfield, Brian, 1963–
    Ring of fire : a tribute to Johnny Cash / Brian Mansfield ; photographs by
Les Leverett.
      p. cm.
    ISBN 1-4016-0137-5
      1. Cash, Johnny. 2. Country musicians—United States—Biography.
    I. Leverett, Les. II. Title.
    ML420.C265M35 2004
    782.421642'092—DC22

                        2003020931

Printed in the United States of America

03 04 05 06 07 — 5 4 3 2 1

PREFACE

MANY MEN BECOME LEGENDS after their death. Few become myths during their lifetimes.

Johnny Cash was such a man.

The simple mention of his name evokes an unforgettable picture in the mind—craggy features that seem cut from stone, deep-set eyes that smolder with ancient fire, dark garb that cloaks him in both symbol and mystery.

During a career spanning a half century, Cash meant many things to many people. There was Cash the rockabilly and Cash the country boy. Cash the cowboy and Cash the outlaw. Cash the rebel and Cash the prisoner's friend. Cash the folk singer and Cash the rock 'n' roll icon. Cash the junkie and Cash the wise elder.

Cash, the Man in Black.

Legends often spring up around celebrities after their deaths, once they're no longer around to disprove or disavow the attributes that people project onto them. James Dean, Marilyn Monroe, Jim Morrison, Elvis Presley, John Lennon—they all became larger-than-life figures.

Cash was seen as poet, patriot, preacher, and protester. He absorbed the images the way black absorbs light. He was all those things—and, by being the sum of them, he became something entirely different. Cash, with his overpowering presence, was large enough to encompass such paradoxes.

Cash lent himself to myths. He never shot a man in Reno just to watch him die, but when people hear him sing "Folsom Prison Blues," it's sure easy for them to believe he did. He never did time in prison, but just try convincing the audiences on *Live at Folsom Prison* and *Live at San Quentin* that he wasn't one of their own. He was the kind of guy who could confront authority head-on. When radio wouldn't play his single "The Ballad of Ira Hayes," he took out a full-page ad in *Billboard*, demanding of programmers, "Where are your guts?"—and came out victorious. He took "Ring of Fire," a song by his future wife about her feelings for him, and turned it into a universal statement of love and desire, of love that threatens both to consume and to purify. In his seventh decade, he took a song about addiction—Nine Inch Nails' "Hurt"—and transformed it into a commentary on physical and spiritual frailty.

The people who knew Cash best tell of a flesh-and-blood man behind the icon. They talk unfailingly of astounding generosity, a love of simplicity, and a sense of humor that could border on the absurd. But even those closest to him easily slip into the language of myth when describing him. Kris Kristofferson may have captured his essence in his song "The Pilgrim: Chapter 33." "He's a walking contradiction, partly truth and partly fiction."

The author Nicholas Falletta has described a paradox as "truth standing on its head to attract attention." Cash, always a seeker of truth, stood American popular music on its head by singing songs that come from seemingly unlikely places and by championing people from apparently incompatible walks of life.

He sang the songs of A. P. Carter, Jimmie Rodgers, Thomas Dorsey, Leadbelly, Hank Williams, Woody Guthrie, the Beatles, the Rolling Stones, Bob Dylan, Neil Diamond, Simon & Garfunkel, Bruce Springsteen, Tom Petty, U2, Depeche Mode, Soundgarden, Nine Inch Nails. His catalog of recordings encompassed the American West and the hills of Appalachia, Tin Pan Alley and Music Row, "Rock of Ages" and rock 'n' roll. Perhaps no other singer in the history of American music has sung songs from such disparate sources as Cash, and over such a long period of time. And Cash always made each one of them his own.

Did he contradict himself? Very well, then, as Walt Whitman might have said of him, he contradicted himself. He was large. He contained multitudes.

He was, after all, Johnny Cash.

ACKNOWLEDGMENTS

WITHOUT THE frequent input and advice of Kelly Hancock at the House of Cash, I cannot imagine this book ever would have been finished. Kelly had many more pressing things to do than talk to me, but she always made time for lengthy conversations. Kindness and generosity, apparently, are traits that run deep in the Cash family.

"Cowboy" Jack Clement, Merle Kilgore, and Marty Stuart provided many helpful contacts and references, as did my colleagues Elysa Gardner, Edna Gundersen, and Jaan Uhelski.

Others who offered time and assistance include Earl Poole Ball, Darlene Bieber, Kay Clary, Tom Cording, Emily Deaderick, Braxton Dixon, Michael Figlio, Kim Fowler, Wendell Goodman, Amy Grant, Jeff Hanna, Wynonna Judd, Anita Mandell, Bob Merlis, Jackie Monaghan, Mary Moyer, Jimmy C. Newman, Maureen O'Connor, Randy Pitts, Mark Pucci, Tresa Redburn, Lou Robin, Gaynell Rogers, Nancy Russell, Michael Ruthig, Carla Sacks, Tamara Saviano, Jessie Schmidt, Mitch Schneider, Earl Scruggs, Ricky Skaggs, William Smithson, Susan Swan, Wes Vause, Kirt Webster, and Jules Wortman. Thanks to my editor, Bryan Curtis, for the opportunity and to my wife, Nancy, for waiting to have the baby until I'd turned in the first draft.

Ring of Fire

Marty Stuart

THERE'S TWO KINDS of people. There's those who like Johnny Cash and those that will.

Kris Kristofferson

HE LOOKED LIKE Abraham Lincoln—
if Abraham Lincoln had a dark, wild streak.
His face ought to be up on Mount
Rushmore.

Tommy Cash

BROTHER

WHEN I WAS six years old, he taught me how to swim. The Tyronza River in Dyess, Arkansas, was where we swam, at a big place called the "Blue Hole"—very deep water, and crystal clear. Daddy told him, "Take your little brother down to the river and teach him how to swim."

Johnny said, "Aw, I don't want to, Daddy, I'm going off with my pals."

"Take your little brother down there; teach him how to swim."

Well, I thought he would set me at the edge of the water and let me start dog-paddling. But he threw me off the bridge. It looked like forty feet, but it was probably eight or ten. Then he jumped in the water and got me.

It scared me to death, but I learned to swim real quick.

CASH WITH JIMMY C. NEWMAN.

Charlie Louvin

WE PLAYED John's hometown—or the closest thing to his hometown. I believe it was Dyess, Arkansas. At the time, I was eighteen, so he would've been twelve and a half or thirteen. We got to this school a little late, and people had already gone in and sat down. We had to run the people out so I could sell the tickets.

There was one little guy standing outside in a pair of overalls with no shirt on and no shoes and the awfulest tan you've ever seen in your life. You couldn't have stuck him with an ice pick; his hide looked like it was so tanned that it would be impenetrable.

When I finished selling the tickets, I asked him, "Is there a rest room?" He practically led me to it—it was an outside job. He waited outside, and I came out. I reached in my pocket and got a package of soda crackers. I was eating these crackers on the way back to the schoolhouse. He said, "Why are you eating those soda crackers?" I'm sure I came off like a smart-ass; I said, "To keep from starving to death."

He put in his book that for the first three or four years he was trying to get in the business, he always ate a soda cracker before going on the stage. Which would have been the most damaging thing you could've done to your voice. You can't get rid of it unless you've got some water. When he wrote that in the book, I remembered that little boy with the great tan. And that was Johnny Cash.

Dwight Yoakam

CASH, AS WELL AS other men in his generation, were the post–World War II occupational GIs throughout Europe and Asia. They kind of all evolved into the hillbilly cats through their exposure to the world.

Cash was in Berlin in the early '50s. It's almost like the expatriate jazz musicians that would go to Europe, or the African American players that went over there in the '20s and '30s. They became exposed to European culture in a way that was unique to them. That shaped a generation of musicians. This shaped, also, a generation of guys.

CASH WITH LOUIS ARMSTRONG.

Marshall Grant

CASH'S BASS PLAYER, 1955–1980

THAT OLD awkward sound we had—the first eight bars we ever played in our life, that sound was there. Just there, right then. We spent the next week trying to get rid of it. But we couldn't. And thank God we didn't.

Wanda Jackson

IN 1955, I GUESS IT WAS, when I
started working on shows with Elvis,
Johnny was on quite a few of those shows.
Elvis and I would stand in the wings of the
stage. He thought Johnny was the greatest.
He always caught his shows. He said,
"You see that guy there? He's going to be
the biggest thing that's ever hit the
music industry."

BROTHER

WHEN HIS first record came out, I was fifteen. I was a basketball player, and I was the star of the Dyess, Arkansas, junior high basketball team. We won the state championship that year.

All of us went from being who we were—I was Tommy Cash, the little basketball star, and Mom and Daddy were just the Cashes of Dyess—to being Johnny Cash's family. Instead of people saying, "Oh, Tommy, I saw you play basketball the other night and make twenty-eight points," they'd say, "Are you really Johnny Cash's brother?" That's when it started.

Once I realized—which didn't take but a few months—that he was going to be a big star, my chest just swelled with pride. I thought it was the greatest thing that had ever happened in our lives.

Back then, I had not gone through all the years I've gone through now, answering questions about John. Everywhere I go, even to this day, people say, "Are you really Johnny Cash's brother?" I've grown sort of tired of that.

It changed all of us. But we were all extremely proud of him.

Rodney Crowell

I WAS GOING FISHING one day, in this borrowed '49 Ford my dad used to nick off of a guy. It had one of those big dashboard radios. We were driving in the pre-dawn hours in one of those two-rut roads in the summertime, where the grass was high and the road was just two tire tracks. I was five years old, sleepyheaded, sitting on the back seat with my chin resting on the back of the front seat.

Then, out of nowhere, "I Walk the Line" came on. It just reached over there and got me, just the sound and the words and the way it all came so strangely. You see those stories where someone is taken away to a spaceship? It seemed like that song abducted me out the car. I remember having this thought, like, "Wow, where did that come from? I'm going to spend the rest of my life trying to figure this out."

Merle Kilgore

COWRITER, "RING OF FIRE"

WHEN I WAS on the road with Johnny, he'd get two beers and drink 'em as fast as he could, then go on stage. I said, "Johnny, why do you drink those beers that fast before you go on the stage?"

He answered, "They love to see you sweat, man. They love to see a great man sweating."

Billy Walker

JOHNNY AND I worked a lot of dates together
back in the latter part of the '50s. I remember
one tour in 1957, but we were staying at the Hill
Hotel in Omaha, Nebraska, when he bought the
chickens. He and Marshall Grant and Luther
Perkins bought five hundred baby chickens.
They let a hundred of the chickens out on each
floor of the Hill Hotel. I don't think the hotel
ever found out who, exactly, did it.

Another place we went to, they bought a
bunch of cherry bombs. They was lighting these
cherry bombs and flushing them down the toi-
let. They would go down to the next floor and
blow out the pipes in the plumbing.

Then there was one hotel where they
painted the room black and then cut off the legs
off all the furniture to make it a Japanese room.
They had to pay several hundred dollars for
that deal.

CASH WITH EDWIN CRAIG, FOUNDER OF WSM.

Dolly Parton

I WAS A very young girl, maybe twelve or thirteen, the first time that I saw Johnny Cash on stage at the Grand Ole Opry. He affected me in a way that no male ever had. It stirred my whole being . . . his mannerisms and his low voice. I realized later that it was charisma, but to me it was just pure sex appeal. He has continued to affect me that way throughout his whole career. He's the John Wayne of country music to me.

CASH PERFORMING WITH ROBBIE HARDIN AND MAYBELLE, HELEN, AND ANITA CARTER.

Brenda Lee

ONE OF HIS MOST endearing qualities is
his ability to speak to the common man.
Not only to speak, but to write poignantly
about the common man and the problems
that people in America truly face, and to
commiserate with that, truthfully and
honestly from his heart.

Loretta Lynn

JOHNNY'D WALK OUT on stage where
nobody could see him. He'd walk sideways,
kind of, then get out there with his back
toward the audience. He'd keep his head
hid, and then he'd turn around and say,
"Hello, I'm Johnny Cash." The place
would go up.

Every now and then, I still do that.
I just turn around and say, "Hello, I'm
Johnny Cash."

"Cowboy" Jack Clement

PRODUCER, MUSICIAN, FRIEND

HE'S GOT THE most amazing recording voice that I know of, in terms of getting on the tape. There's what you call apparent level, and then there's actual level. He has this apparent level that just gets on the tape. It's a commodity. You just can't hardly cover it up.

It's almost impossible to drown him out. You can put in lots of drums, horns, a roomful of guitars and everything else— he still cuts through. It's powerful. There's few voices I've ever heard like that. It just flows out and goes right on the tape. I've been calling him Captain Decibel for years because of that.

Guy Clark

HIS WRITING is just stunning. That was
the thing I was always after him to do, to
write more of his own songs. His voice is
unique, and his take is unique. Songs like
"Five Feet High and Rising"? That's an amazing piece of writing, as is "I Walk the Line."

"I Walk the Line," it just sounds like the
simplest thing in the world, but it's really
not. It's really a fairly difficult song to play
and sing at the same time. To actually play
it on guitar and sing it is kind of like patting
your head and rubbing your stomach.

George Jones

JOHNNY CASH is more to me than just an entertainer—he's one of the best friends I've ever had. Johnny doesn't say those things out loud, but the things he does secretly are some of the nicest things that a person can do.

When Johnny was at his peak, he'd give guys like me, Stonewall Jackson, Johnny Western, Skeeter Davis, and the Statler Brothers a lot of work when we were beginning our careers. He did things like that for artists and never said one word about it.

I knew he was doing it to put together a big show, but as hot as he was at the time, he didn't really need that many people. I know he did it to help us.

Braxton Dixon

NASHVILLE DEVELOPER, FRIEND

JOHNNY CASH came out to talk to me about building him a house. We started talking about him wanting to come to Hendersonville and look at some property. We headed out toward the lake, where I was working on my own house. As we approached the building, where he could look and see, he said, "What's that over there?" I said, "That's what I want to show you—that's not for sale, it's my house." I'd been working on it for three or four years.

We went out on the hillside and just sat on the ground there for a minute. He said, "I want to buy it." I said, "John, it's not for sale." I think he made a remark, "Everything somewhere is for sale at some time or other." He said there was no need for him to do any building, he wanted to buy that. He'd make one offer, and I'd say no, and he'd make another one. At some point, I said, "Well, you just bought yourself a house." And we've been friends ever since.

PERFORMER, SIDEMAN, DISC JOCKEY

WHEN JUNE CARTER and the Carter
Family came along on the tours, Johnny
hired the entire Carter Family. Of course,
he and June started looking at each other
across the microphone. The sparks were
definitely starting to heat up. That whole
thing started right there, and from there
on there was no other girl singer on
his shows.

It overwhelmed everybody. Gordon
Terry and I could see it coming on. We
would look at each other, shake our heads
and say, "This thing is coming on like a
truckload of turkeys." You just knew.

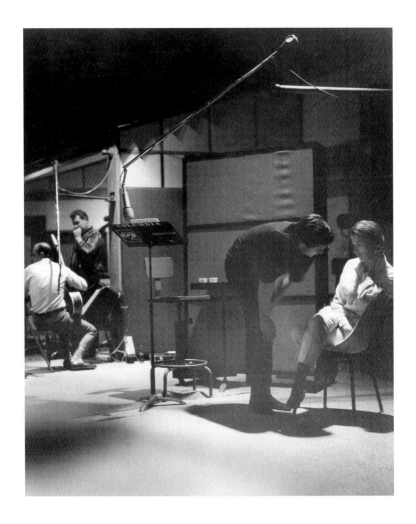

JUNE CARTER CASH'S COUSIN

JOHN AND JUNE always seemed like the ideal couple. They always seemed so concerned, or foolish, about one another. You can really tell if it's make-believe or put-on or the real thing. Theirs was the real, real thing. They seemed very devoted to one another. The way he'd speak to her, in a kind voice. Anything she wanted, why, it was all right, she could go ahead and do it. He just seemed to want to give her things all the time, and she was awful kind and good to him. They seemed very suited to one another.

June Carter Cash

I CHOSE TO BE Mrs. Johnny Cash in my life. I decided I'd allow him to be Moses, and I'd be Moses' brother Aaron, picking his arms up and padding along behind him. I stayed in submission to my husband, and he allowed me to do anything I wanted to. I felt like I was lucky to have that kind of romance.

Marty Stuart

I ALWAYS GO BACK to what Solomon said in the Bible. Solomon had the greatest of everything, and, at the end of it all, he counted it all but vanity. It's a powerful lesson to look at somebody like me that's still chasing and running, trying to do the right thing and make the moves and play music and make a difference. It's quite another thing to see somebody in John's position, who has accomplished it all and has made the victory lap and would trade every bit of it in to touch her hand one more time. Would count every bit of that worthless, just to hold somebody's hand and be loved one more time. It sends you home to think.

Ramblin' Jack Elliott

I WAS ON the Johnny Cash TV show as a guest a couple of times. The first time I was on was the very second show they ever did in 1969. The first one, the guest was Bob Dylan.

I visited John out on the lake. We went fishing. We were out in the boat, and John says, "Hey, Jack, are you going to go to this Woodstock thing?"

I said, "What Woodstock thing?" I hadn't heard about it.

He said, "I don't know what it is, but Bob sent me a letter. He cautioned me not to come. He didn't want me to come because he didn't want to get a big crowd there in his hometown."

"Oh," I said, "well, if you're not going, I ain't going, either. That's settled."

CASH WITH LINDA RONSTADT.

Stan Jacobson

PRODUCER, *The Johnny Cash Show*

[MERLE TRAVIS AND JOHN] were out
in a boat on some lake. These were the
days, Merle said, when they were popping
pills and drinking. John stood up in the
boat, and it was kind of choppy water.
It was like a little rowboat, I think. Merle
said, "You better sit down; you may fall off
and drown." Johnny said, "I can't fall off
and drown; I'm a legend."

CASH PERFORMING WITH MARSHALL GRANT, CARL PERKINS,
AND JUNE, ANITA, AND HELEN CLARK.

Kris Kristofferson

I HAD KNOWN John for almost two years. I had pitched him every song that I ever wrote while I was working at Columbia. He had invited me to his house, but he never had cut a song of mine.

I was in the Tennessee National Guard for a brief time, trying to earn money to support my family. We flew these old helicopters that were about to fall out of the sky. You had to fly so much just to get paid every month, and on one of my flights I decided I would take a tape over there and just drop in on his lawn.

As it happened, I almost landed on top of his house. I was just lucky he didn't blow me out of the sky. I have to admit, I was hoping it would make an impression on him.

He tells me that it was "Sunday Morning Coming Down," and that's why he recorded it. I don't exactly remember it that way, but I'm willing to go along with John's memory, which is at least as good as mine.

That story comes back to haunt me all the time, because people feel they can invade my privacy in any way they want, because at least it's not in a helicopter. And they say so.

CASH AT A RECORDING SESSION WITH LUTHER PERKINS AND RAY EDDINGTON.

BROTHER

IN 1976, I DID a whole year with *The Johnny Cash Show*.
I opened and emceed the show during the bicentennial year.
It was the Carters and myself and sometimes Carl Perkins,
sometimes Gordon Terry, and sometimes other people on
the show.

We were at the University of Wisconsin—I think at the
Eau Claire branch. I was in the dressing room with John,
which was the men's locker room. I saw him walking up and
down the aisles, looking into the lockers. The lockers had
little square holes where you could look in the top of them
and see what was in the locker.

I saw him looking, and I said, "What are you doing?"
He said, "Aw, nothin'." Then I saw him stop, roll up a bill, put
it through a hole, and drop it into somebody's tennis shoes.
I said, "What did you do?" He said, "Well, it doesn't matter."
I said, "No, tell me. What were you doing?" He said, "Well, I
was looking for the guy that had the oldest, raggediest tennis
shoes and gym clothes. I dropped a hundred-dollar bill in his
tennis shoes."

CASH PERFORMING WITH CARL PERKINS.

Rodney Crowell

I MET Johnny Cash's wrath—and there's a lot of it—as a young man. It also deflated my arrogant stance that I thought I had to make to prove that I was somebody.

I was living with his daughter Rosanne in Los Angeles. I was paying the rent and everything, but this was not sanctioned, living in sin with his daughter. We received a summons to Jamaica in the form of two airline tickets. I knew what was up, so I drank the whole way. I was not presentable when I got there and not in possession of my wits, either.

When we got to their place up in Cinnamon Hill, I overheard Rosanne, kind of teary. She was in this conversation with her dad in his room. I wanted John and June to think I was my own man and I wasn't just digging around this family. So I went in, and I said, "John, we live together, and I'd be a hypocrite if I didn't say that's what we should do."

Boy, he looked at me—just fixed me—and he said, "Son, I don't know you well enough to miss you if you were to leave."

Marty Stuart

THEY STOPPED US at the Russian border. He got his guitar out, at their request, and hit a lick. They all applauded. At a McDonald's in Berlin, he caused a stir. I saw everything from a little boy coming backstage in Kansas and asking him to pull his tooth to a prisoner's mom getting down on her hands and knees, wrapping her arms around his calves, and begging him to get her boy off of death row. I saw it all. It's amazing what God gave him.

I think he knows what Johnny Cash means to the world. He's humble about it, but he's a master showman, too. Never forget that.

Brenda Lee

WHEN MY CHILD was desperately ill,
Johnny and June Carter came forward and
visited and started a prayer chain for her.
They kept a vigil for her until she got well.
That was a wonderful thing to do.

Ricky Skaggs

HIS GRACIOUSNESS and humility almost brought me to tears. He's been down the road. He's really been down the road. He's a prime example of God's grace, how good it is.

CASH WITH BILLY GRAHAM.

John Carter Cash

SON

HE WAS ALWAYS a tender man, always a gentle man, and loving. He always was open, considerate, forgiving. His heart was always there, in answer to any need. He was never angry.

Down through the years, he was consistent as a spiritual rock, in touch with God. He had tenacity and resilience like no other human I know, the way he bounced back.

My father never tried to force any direction on me, as far as career, as far as "this is what you must do for a living." My father always let me figure things out for myself. He would back me and stand beside me in what I believed in and the things that I wanted to do. He was always there for me. He didn't offer a lot of advice, unless you asked him.

He told me down through the years that I can accomplish anything that I set my dreams to, that I set within my vision.

EMPLOYEE

HE'S GOT 106 ACRES down here in Bon Aqua, Tennessee. It's got an old log house on it, and I guess the house is over a hundred years old. When him and June walked in the old log house, they knew right then they wanted to keep it, and they wanted to keep it just like it was. They kept it like it was for years, without any central heat and air in it. It had fireplaces, and I cut wood for the fires. He didn't want to put central heat and air in, because he wanted to smell that smoke and see it burn.

He just loved to come down there and walk, walk over the place. He had a Jeep that he kept down there for a long time. Used to, we'd just ride the back roads. Him and June and the kids would get out and ride the back roads, talk to people, just like one of the people.

He got to coon hunting with me. He loved to coon hunt. I took him and my two little boys—John Carter was just a little boy—coon hunting. When we'd kill a coon, John would bring it home and eat it. I would dress it for him, and they'd bring it home and have it cooked.

John Mellencamp

THE MOST embarrassing moment of my career happened on stage with Johnny Cash. I was playing at the show when they opened up the Rock and Roll Hall of Fame building. I performed with a couple people, and Cash was one of them.

The night before, I could tell John was getting a little irritated with the sound check going long. We had to do "Ring of Fire," and he said, "Do you want to go over this?" I said, "I got it." He said, "You sure?" I could tell he wanted to get out of there, and I kind of wanted to get out of there, too. It was, like, three hours into it, and I didn't want to be there. So I said, "I got it, I got it, I got it." And I knew the song.

We walked out on stage the next day, and every contemporary guy in the rock business was watching from the side of the stage with Johnny Cash. Everybody loves Johnny Cash. So we start "Ring of Fire," and then I realize that Cash guy's voice is much deeper than mine. So I had to go real low. I thought, that isn't going to work, so I went up real high. Cash looks down at me, and he just kind of closes his eyes.

After it was over, I saw all my contemporaries looking at me, mortified. And there's eighty thousand people out there. And it's on television, going around the world.

As we walked off stage, Cash looks at me and he goes, "I told you we should've rehearsed."

Dave Roe

CASH'S BASS PLAYER, 1992–2003

SOMEONE TOLD HIM I was the best rockabilly slap-bass player in the world.

I'd never played rockabilly slap bass in my life. I hadn't touched an upright bass in twenty years. But I took a shot at it and went out there.

He came up to me after the show and said, "You don't really play this stuff, do you?" I said, "Nope." He said, "Well, what'd you come out here for?" I said, "Now I can say I played with Johnny Cash." He started laughing, and he turned around and said, "I'll give you six months. If you can learn this stuff, you can stay here a long time."

Not only did it get me the gig and keep me the gig, it changed my life. I went from being a regular old electric bass player to somebody who's a lot more. Because I played with Johnny Cash.

TOM PETTY & THE HEARTBREAKERS

OF ALL THE THINGS I've done, when my mom and dad heard I'd worked with Johnny, it was like, forget everything else, you've made it now, kid.

CASH WITH GARY BUCK *(standing, left)* AND BOB LUMAN *(standing, right)*.

Ira Dean

TRICK PONY

JOHNNY'S ONE OF the few guys that
you can feel walk into a room before you
see him. You can have your back to the
door and know he walked through it.

Trisha Yearwood

I WILL NEVER FORGET the first time I met Johnny Cash. It was through the mail! It was 1992, and I had just released my second album, *Hearts in Armor.* I was getting ready to hit the road on tour and was doing hundreds of interviews to promote the record and the tour dates.

One show was to be in Branson, Missouri, and I was interviewing with one of the local newspapers there when the journalist asked me, "What makes you think people will come to see your show when there are so many legendary country music artists performing on the same night?" I thought about it for a second, and out of my mouth came the most honest answer I could think of. "Well, I don't know," I said. "If Johnny Cash was performing on the same night I was, I think I'd go see him!"

I didn't give it another thought until a few weeks later when a letter arrived at my home in Nashville from the House of Cash. Inside was the interview I had given with the quote about Mr. Cash highlighted, and a handwritten letter from the Man in Black himself! Well, I can remember my heart pounding, and I can remember leaning up against the wall in the kitchen and sliding down to the floor as I read his letter.

He thanked me for my comments and then told me that he liked my music, in particular the single that I had out at the time, "Wrong Side of Memphis." I had been a fan of his music all my life, but that kind letter in the beginning of my career made me a fan of the man. It's one of the most treasured memories of my career.

CASH WITH RECORD SHOP OWNER LOUIS BUCKLEY AND A FAN.

Merle Haggard

WE SPENT some time together recently
on a recording session. We'd finished
recording, and we were out in the woods
near his studio, talking about everything.

I said, "Tell me something. You probably know: How did Roy Acuff hold that gig
all those years, singing out of key?"

He'd been just talking normal up till
then, but he turned and looked at me, and
he got that Johnny Cash voice. He said,
"Evidently, you haven't heard. Roy Acuff
could whip anybody on the Opry, includ-
ing Bill Monroe. He whipped Bill Monroe
twice. That's the reason Roy Acuff was the
king of country."

Dwight Yoakam

HE WAS the true, and probably the only, lasting rockabilly act. Cash represented that bridge between being a rock and a hillbilly artist. He was the only one that was a lasting example of it in a successful way. Cash clearly achieved great success in doing it. Because of that, and his staying the course, he became a category unto himself. People say, "I never considered Johnny Cash country, just Johnny Cash."

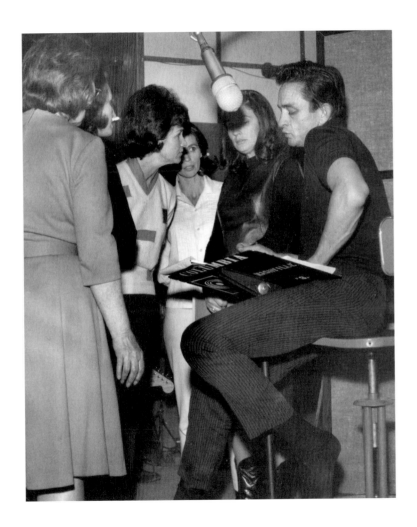

Tom Petty

JOHNNY CASH crossed into rock 'n' roll by that rebellious attitude. He lived his life so on the wild side, there for so long. I think that's where he certainly gained the respect of the rock 'n' roll crowd. He was as dangerous as Keith Richards ever was.

And he was honest. That's the word that always comes up to me. Honesty, that rings true. If you bring that to your music, that'll ring true across all genres of music.

NINE INCH NAILS

RICK RUBIN called me up and asked, "How would you feel about Johnny Cash recording 'Hurt'?" My first reaction was that I was flattered, but it seemed wrong. I'd written the song in my bedroom, out of my personal pain. I'd never considered myself a songwriter—it was a way to keep my sanity. It seemed kind of strange. When I got the song back, it seemed really strange. But not in a bad way. This was my creation, upended into something else. I didn't listen to it much at first.

When Rick sent me the video, that's when it hit home. That's when the goose bumps set in. It made me appreciate how powerful music can be. Here was that rebellious, tormented, pain-laden persona—singing my words back to me. That put it in a completely different perspective. It removed me from the equation. Now it was his song.

It surprised me that it could function so well, that it could be adapted to this setting, and that it would be just as powerful, if not more so. When I watch the video, I get goose bumps. When I hear the song, I get choked up.

MUSICIAN

THE LAST TIME I was out there, it was
the most focused he'd been in a long time.
His focus had gotten stronger, literally,
week by week. Physically, it was difficult,
because he had a difficult time with the
walker. He needed at least that, just to go a
few steps. Normally, he would have someone that would help him out in the car, he
would have a walker to get in, and there
would be a wheelchair. That was just to
keep him mobile. It wasn't like he was
attached to the wheelchair.

I could tell his voice was getting
stronger. And the last time, he did great
vocals. I could still see such a creative spark.
It was more than a spark. It was like a
creative fire.

Marty Stuart

TWO TRAIN-RIDIN' VULTURES have taken up residence right outside the window of his office. They stare at him, and he stares back. And he *likes* them.

It takes a guy pretty secure in his position in the world to befriend vultures.